Prayers
for Your
Newborn

Noah benShea

SOURCEBOOKS, INC.®
NAPERVILLE, ILLINOIS

Published by Sourcebooks, Inc.
P.O. Box 4410, Naperville, Illinois   60567-4410
(630) 961-3900
Fax: (630) 961-2168
www.sourcebooks.com

Library of Congress Cataloging-in-Publication Data
BenShea, Noah.
 Prayers for your newborn / Noah benShea.
   p. cm.
 ISBN-13: 978-1-4022-0658-0
 ISBN-10: 1-4022-0658-5
1. Parents—Prayer-books and devotions—English. 2. Infants (Newborn)—Prayer-books and devotions—English. I. Title.

BL625.8.B46 2005
204'.33085—dc22

                              2005025022

                    Printed and bound in China.
                    LEO 10 9 8 7 6 5 4 3 2 1

"Prayer is a path where there is none."

—Noah benShea

This book is dedicated
to every parent's prayer
for every child,
and to my children
Jordan Arin and Adam Joseph
in whom
God has answered my prayers.

Dear Parent,

Parenting is a process that moves from management to consultant, if we're lucky. Consequently if we want to wrap our arms around our children, wrapping them in prayers may be our best option.

Prayers, like angels' wings, can shelter our children from life's storms, and wing them to places where parents may only dream their child will ever visit.

Here are some prayers you might want to whisper to your child when they are young, and remind them when they are older, and once again when they are older yet. They will be forever your child, and you will be forever their parent. And in the forever of things, perhaps this book will one day be theirs.

My own prayer for your child is this:

> May you go from strength to strength
> and be a source of strength to others.

Parent to parent, know you are in my prayers.

Noah benShea

Dear Child...

May we welcome you to the human race
and remind you that it is not a race.

Dear Child...

May you learn to find peace not in what
you are given, but in who you are.

Dear Child...

May you come to know that you are gifted
because you have been given the gift of life.

Dear Child...

May you remember that courage is fear
that has said its prayers,
and remember to say yours.

Dear Child...

May you come to know that the greatest
love you can give your parents
will be for you to love your children.

Dear Child...

May you always remember that
fear knocks at every door,
but when faith answers
there is no one there.

Dear Child...

May you listen to the bird outside your
window who can teach you to wake up
every morning with a song in your heart.

Dear Child...

May you remember that if you want to
feel better, say a prayer for someone who
needs to feel better.

Dear Child...

May you learn while you are young that
you can't save time; you can only spend it,
and life's treasure is in how you spend it.

Dear Child...

May you learn while you are young that
the best way to save a moment is to savor it.

Dear Child...

May you remember all you can about
your first love so you can have their
company when you grow old.

Dear Child...

May you discover sooner rather than later that doing a good deed makes it a good day.

Dear Child...

May you see your shadow as a reminder
that you are blessed to have the sun
shining on you.

Dear Child...

May you remember that our spirit grows
homesick when we don't come home to
who we really are.

Dear Child...

May you come to know that in every dark forest there is one bird that knows your name and keeps calling it out so you will find your way.

Dear Child...

May you learn that the walls you felt you needed to protect you also support your fears, and your fears support your need for walls.

Dear Child...

May you never forget to visit the opinions of others, even as you know where your own opinions call home.

Dear Child...

May you be honest with people who give you their anger, and give it back without making it yours.

Dear Child...

May you learn sooner than later that
we're often in the dark only because
we've shut our eyes.

Dear Child...

May you witness that we can be both
blinded by success or achieve failure
because of what we refuse to see.

Dear Child...

May you immunize yourself by learning
that the need for approval can be an
addiction, and self-approval is the cure.

Dear Child...

May you come to realize that while roses
have thorns, thorns can also have roses.

Dear Child...

May you come to realize that the only
thing that will hold you back more than
ignorance is the illusion of knowledge.

Dear Child...

May you greet each day knowing that
you are as young as your hopes and as
old as your fears.

Dear Child...

May you never forget that you can make things turn out better if you make the best of how things turn out.

Dear Child...

May you take a little time each day to
bend your pride, stretch your hopes, and
reach to touch inwardly what was
beyond your grasp yesterday.

Dear Child...

May you discover that real wealth is
gratitude for what you have.

Dear Child...

May you stop and notice something every
day that you did not notice the day before,
and notice the change in you.

Dear Child...

May you have friends who can grow with
you, and, like you, are amazed about
growing old.

Dear Child...

May you never allow your past to kidnap
your future.

Dear Child...

May you learn to laugh at yourself so that
your life will never lack amusement.

Dear Child...

May you be enough of an optimist to
always think you can fly, and enough of a
pessimist to always pack a parachute.

Dear Child...

May you learn sooner rather than later
that the more your life's a rush, the sooner
it's a blur.

Dear Child...

May you discover the peace that comes
from learning to respond, not react.

Dear Child...

May you say your prayers not because
you should but because you can.

Dear Child...

May you be committed to being your best,
and achieve it by trying each day to be a
little better.

Dear Child...

May you never forget that few things are
sadder than the person whose next train
in life is the one that left ten minutes ago.

Dear Child...

May you remember that what's true can make for a good story, but a good story is its own truth.

Dear Child...

May you understand that what you give
someone may be very different than what
they take from it.

Dear Child...

May you learn that many stumble over the truth, but too many hurry on as if nothing had happened.

Dear Child...

May you learn that what can trip you up
can be the trip of a lifetime.

Dear Child...

May you enjoy the praise of others, but
may you learn the difference between
what you enjoy and what you need.

Dear Child...

May you treasure the quiet that comes
from quieting your own noise.

Dear Child...

When you think you have seen it all, may
you come to discover how blind you
have been.

Dear Child...

May you discover that the highest calling
of self-interest can be responding to the
call of another.

Dear Child...

May you lift the veil through which you've been taught to see the world, kiss the moment, and wed the uncensored day.

Dear Child...

May you dress for the day without
wearing someone else's emotional clothing.

Dear Child...

May you discover that what fits you best
is being your best.

Dear Child...

May you come to realize that even in the
wonders of a multicolor world, there are
black and white moments of clarity.

Dear Child...

May you recall the carpenter's reminder
to measure twice and cut once;
and know that no matter what you are
making, remembering to do this will
make a difference.

Dear Child...

May you never try to hold a five-foot
snake with a three-foot stick.

Dear Child...

May you never throw a drowning man ten feet from shore a five-foot rope and tell him you are willing to meet him halfway.

Dear Child...

May you learn that achieving some of
life's greatest feats requires from us a
willingness to go just a few feet further.

Dear Child...

May you have the courage to say what you
stand for, and the grace to then sit down.

Dear Child...

May you remember how much you love
being hugged, and hug someone who
doesn't feel loved.

Dear Child...

May you always listen to what others say
and what it says about them.

Dear Child...

May you learn from those who you doubt
have anything to teach you, because even
a broken clock is right twice a day.

Dear Child...

May you always be prepared to trade
being right for doing right.

Dear Child...

May you learn that you will never be able
to read people until you learn to read
between the lines.

Dear Child...

May you find your cup half-full when it is half-empty.

Dear Child...

May you learn the real wisdom to make
difficult things simple, and not to make
simple things difficult.

Dear Child...

May you discover the difference between
having to say something and having
something to say.

Dear Child...

May you realize that being a leader is more than a lot of people running around doing what you say.

Dear Child...

May you learn that if you can't swallow
your pride, it will poison you.

Dear Child...

May you not spend your days so
despairing of the wave you missed that
you miss the next wave.

Dear Child...

May you take the time to discover that you
will seldom find the time for anyone or
anything for which you do not
make the time.

Dear Child...

May you remember that pain and fear often appear to be in small doses to those who spoon it out, but never to those who swallow.

Dear Child...

May you never drown in self-pity—even
when the seas are inviting.

Dear Child...

May you always remember that no one
ever found love who wasn't loving.

Dear Child...

May you remember that you are more
likely to have God's company when you
are good company.

Dear Child...

May you be blessed, and say thank you
by being a blessing to others.

Dear Child...

May you never forget that those who take
for granted what they have been given
take too much.

About the Author

Noah benShea is a poet, philosopher, scholar, executive advisor, humorist, and international best-selling author. His books on Jacob the Baker are embraced around the world and have influenced generations. He has been an assistant dean at UCLA, and his work has been included in publications of Oxford University and the World Bible Society in Jerusalem. His weekly inspirational essay, "Noah's Window," has been carried nationally on the *New York Times* regional syndicate and was nominated for a Pulitzer Prize. Mr. benShea's award-winning winning book, *Remember This My Child*, was a finalist for the Gift Book of the Year. He is also the author of *Dear Mom, Dear Dad, Dear Friend,* and *Dear Teacher.*

He is a frequent keynote lecturer who has spoken at the Library of Congress as well as to educators, businesses, and community leaders across North America. Widely interviewed on radio and television, Mr. benShea has two children, lives in Santa Barbara, California, and actually reads the email at his website www.NoahbenShea.com.